POWERS OF CONGRESS

BY ALICE FULTON

Dance Script With Electric Ballerina
Palladium
Powers Of Congress
Sensual Math
Feeling as a Foreign Language: The Good Strangeness of Poetry
Felt

POWERS OF CONGRESS

POEMS

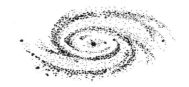

ALICE FULTON

Sarabande Books

LOUISVILLE, KENTUCKY

Managing Editor
Sarabande Books, Inc.
2234 Dundee Road, Suite 200
Louisville, KY 40205

For additional material about this author and this title please visit the *Sarabande
in Education* Website at *http://www.sarabandebooks.org/sie/*. Follow the instructions
on the Website for free access to educational materials.

LIBRARY OF CONGRESS CATALOGING-IN-PUBLICATION DATA

Fulton, Alice.
Powers of Congress / by Alice Fulton.
p.   cm.
ISBN 1-889330-62-0 (alk. paper)

Library of Congress Catalogue Card Number: 90-55275

Cover image: *Still Life Reviving*, 1963, by Remedios Varo. Used by kind
permission of Walter Gruen.

Cover design Hank De Leo

Manufactured in the United States of America.
This book is printed on acid-free paper.

Sarabande Books is a nonprofit literary organization.

First published in 1990 by David R. Godine, Publisher, Inc.

Funded in part by a grant from the Kentucky Arts Council, a state agency of
the Education, Arts, and Humanities Cabinet.

for Hank

CONTENTS

POWERS OF CONGRESS

Cascade Experiment

Because faith creates its verification
and reaching you will be no harder than believing
in a planet's caul of plasma,
or interacting with a comet
in its perihelion passage, no harder
than considering what sparking of the vacuum, cosmological
impromptu flung me here, a paraphrase, perhaps,
for some denser, more difficult being,
a subsidiary instance, easier to grasp
than the span I foreshadow, of which I am a variable,
my stance is passional toward the universe and you.

Because faith in facts can help create those facts,
the way electrons exist only when they're measured,
or shy people stand alone at parties,
attract no one, then go home to feel more shy,
I begin by supposing our attrition's no quicker
than a star's, that like electrons
vanishing on one side
of a wall and appearing on the other
without leaving any holes or being
somewhere in between, the soul's decoupling
is an oscillation so inward nothing outward
as the eye can see it.
The childhood catechisms all had heaven,
an excitation of mist.
Grown, I thought a vacancy awaited me.
Now I find myself discarding and enlarging
both these views, an infidel of amplitude.

Because truths we don't suspect have a hard time
making themselves felt, as when thirteen species
of whiptail lizards composed entirely of females

stay undiscovered due to bias
against such things existing,
we have to meet the universe halfway.
Nothing will unfold for us unless we move toward what
looks to us like nothing: faith is a cascade.
The sky's high solid is anything
but, the sun going under hasn't
budged, and if death divests the self
it's the sole event in nature
that's exactly what it seems.

Because believing a thing's true
can bring about that truth,
and you might be the shy one, lizard or electron,
known only through advances
presuming your existence, let my glance be passional
toward the universe and you.

Disorder Is A Measure Of Warmth

Out of whose womb came the ice? and the hoary
frost of heaven, who hath gendered it?
                                        Job 38:29

In the window, frost forms cradles
                more fail-safe than the beams
        of string kids knit
                between their fingers.

Listening deeply, we might fancy
                infinitesimal clicks
        as each tailored wafer builds
                its strict array,

though the tiny silence
                of the crystal's
        like the giant quiet
                of the heavens in full swing.

No wonder hundreds
                named their daughters Krystal
        after a goblet
                of blond starlet

on TV. Madonna Paradox, she
                forges a perfection
        older than enzyme or ferment
                within the human melo-

drama of protoplasm and cell.
                The rapt nation stares
        at panes that quicken
                with kidnapped infants,

love children, surrogate
        mothers. "Dynasty"
    means wives breeding
        boys to wear men's names

like designer labels
        in greedy immortalities,
    the live-forever-
        land of ads. The coiffed plots,

rote gamut of affairs,
        formulaic chablis evening
    clothes are pleasing
        as snowflakes or crystals:

ignorant things
        that succeed in being
    gorgeous without needing to be
        alive. How deeply we,

the products of chance collisions
        between wrinkled linens,
    full of eccentricity and mission,
        want to be like them.

A Diamond Solitaire

Green shades grew down the panes like moss.
The Callahans recalled the box
and ring. How a certain grandniece dropped
an old engagement stone and they held her
by her heels above the lake to grope.
How lightning split the crystal dish
that rested in the sink.

That Advent in times past, Kit wound her chestnut hair
into a coronet. She lit a vigil light and pledged
devotions: she'd take the altar
linens home to launder, fast before the feast,
give her ring next time the Church sought gold
for chalices if she were spared the childbed fever
marriage brought the mother
she'd never known. At Confirmation,

she'd taken The Kitchen Saint as patron,
vowing to keep house. *Let her spin wool
when she is not praying and pass her time with ancient
virgins* ... Plum conserve. Liturgical
purples lined the pantry.
Let her sisters say their morning mush was cold
and watch her auburn temper smoke.

That damp Advent, Kit crocheted while she waited.
The green hearth was just for show. She pinned
the drapes on racks to dry the pleats. Imagined
gem-set edges on suspended rings of light within
cathedrals. She read about a man removed from slavery
who'd made a lovely casing for the Cup
of the Last Supper. First the fast
then the feast. *The day will pass*

and night will find the child . . .
The porch was dark as horehound drops
when her suitor pressed the bell.
He brought a box of candy.
Kit thought, he promised — I expected —
and struck his hand before he had a chance
to whisper look inside: another box, a ring.

Tell me, O ye professors
of poverty, what does gold do
in a holy place? Kit quoted
to her nieces down the years
while starching the altar linens'
fungal lace, crocheting bags to hold the camphor
they hung around their necks.
Mildewed roses full of ice. She bought herself

a signet ring and said she wanted
a blue sink. Sighing she said
learning comes from books, penetration
of a mystery comes from suffering.
And those who make the nine First Fridays
ascend directly into heaven.
The sisters conferred before confession

and settled on identical sins.
A lady occupies her time by honoring and serving
high personages. They stood on the porch and chorused
audible curtsies of good morning
to Father Carey, a priestly priest,
as he strolled by. Least among least.
Feeling the crossbeams.

Long after it was lost
inside the lake, Kit claimed the diamond
solitaire was found. My yes.

Kieran Fitzpatrick caught a rough gray fish
and found the stone embedded in its flesh.
Let her have as her companion a girl grave

and pale, shabbily dressed, rather sad.
At least one grandniece laughed about the fish.
She said Kieran saw within the algal mess
a crystal wink that was the ring.
And from her deathbed Kit hailed
the Angel Mefathiel, Opener of Doors,
as she had that Advent long ago.

She'd been reading Saint Jerome's instructions
for a nun: *The day will pass*
and night will find the child still
toiling. Let her always be a trifle...
She regretted never getting
her blue sink. *A trifle*
hungry, that was it.

The Orthodox Waltz

Courtship, the seamless mesh
under taffeta havocs
of hoopskirt, smoke

hoops from his Lucky Strikes
her words jumped through.
Women dancing had the harder part,

she'd heard, because they must
dance backward.
He kept his ear pressed

like a safecracker's
stethoscope against
her head, kept his

recombinant endearments
tumbling toward a click.
The lachrymose music,

his clasp and lust-
spiel, displaced her
mother's proverbs. How nimble

they were, those girls
gliding by on dollies.
What had her mother said

that sounded wise? Was it
"Women dancing must be agile
as refugees with jewels

tied to their thighs"?

Self-Storage

"Doesn't that feel great?"
asks Aerobia, Goddess of the Body.
Those muscular curls, ribbons of fire
beneath her skin, give good definition
to the wilderness stashed within.
She's smoothing out the kinks and nicks:
perfection is necessary in a gift.

That's why we dress our presents
in foils and tissues.
Lions lie down with lambs
across each Christmas.
There's a nice democracy to it:
each thing entices equally,
and the trim prolongs the tension
before possession
when lessening begins.
So you want a pet and get
an air conditioner.
From this, you learn to want
what you are given.

When my mother was ill and I was little
I made her a mint jelly sandwich, which she ate
or hid because it was a gift.
The misprisions!
If only we got what we deserved.
In our family, plenty lay naked
beneath the tree on Christmas.
My parents didn't see the sense in wrapping
what we'd only rush to open.
"Let's get down to brass tacks."
That was one of their expressions.

So I was surprised last summer
to receive boxes done in holly wreaths and manger
scenes from home. Thick layers of "invisible"
tape held notes — "2 kitchen towels," "1 nightgown,"
as if to forestall false hopes.
The only mystery was my mother's candor.
And I was mystified at Christmas
to find she'd wrapped presents
for herself, even tagging them "For Mary."

But all the gifts dropped like hints
of what the giver wants
can't change the fact
of who is giving.
Whether roses come from boss or lover's
a distinction like that
between epidermis and skin.
"Though dadgummit," pants the Goddess,
"there's a point — lift...three...two...
one... — where it gets compulsive."

And where's that? Where
buyers spend big bucks on little nothings
at the cut-rate malls?
"We cash checks," each chain implores.
Last Christmas while shopping
I stood still, watching snow
machines forge the hills
to calendar art. "Michigan Collision"
stood beside "Self-Storage:"
cubes holding the dislocated
against fire or theft. Near the freeway
where cars whisked by
like sweepings, the goods
and I stood to just one side.
A child swathed in floral layers
touched my hand

at last like something up for sale.
"That's not a fake lady," her mother
said, pulling her away.

Personally, I prefer gifts too big to wrap:
the inflammatory abstracts, say —
love, forgiveness, faith —
that sear through any paper
so packaging them's like tucking
flames into tuxedos.

Maybe all presents are presumptions.
Giving, we test our affinity
with hidden wishes. Yet asking
changes both desire and deliverance,
as when lovers must say touch me
there. No matter.
Some things we'd gladly have
from any hand. Give us this day
in the pliable rain,
a solitude unlike a lidded wilderness,
a soft death — now doesn't that feel great?

I wouldn't say so. No.
What we want is another and another
day rising behind firm skylines,
a pink ridge shining into brick.
But when wasn't *always* not
less with dawn? Oh bright box
ripping in its own good time —

Powers Of Congress

How the lightstruck trees change sun
to flamepaths: veins, sap, stem, all
on brief loan, set to give all
their spooled, coded heat to stoves called
Resolute: wet steel die-cast
by heat themselves. Tree, beast, bug —
the world-class bit parts in this
world — flit and skid through it; the
powers of congress tax, spend, law
what lives to pure crisp form
then break forms' lock, stock, and hold
on flesh. All night couples pledge
to stay flux, the hit-run stuff
of cracked homes. Men trim their quick
lawns each weekend, trailing power
mowers. Heartslaves, you've seen them: wives
with flexed hair, hitched to bored kids,
twiddling in good living rooms,
their twin beds slept in, changed, made.

Hardware

I don't know how this silk-screened memory
expansion board — its soldered subdivisions
exposed yet unembarrassed as a city seen from air —
holds a million bytes that flame
to words when touched, but it does.

It sits on my desk like a skull
or a phone, another sculpted composure.
I like a phone because I can hold it
and join the circumference
of radial cables that bind
the earth's hot core with voice.
And I know a touch that sends it
on a global search to snare the line
I need, immediately.
Technology is something

to rely on when your clothes catch fire,
as mine did all last year.
I don't know how the everyday selvage
from my closet became a conflagration,
but what a spectacle I made
in my candescent dress!
Trying to run from what consumed me
only urged it on.

When my friend said, "Hold still,
I'll help you out," I was distracted
by a hundred molten buttons.
Wrapped in that emphatic shift,
I lacked self-discipline.
Besides, even a fiery daywear covers
nakedness. Only love can disembarrass one

to strip. When I did
I kept undressing
long after all the clothes were gone.
My skin felt like brimstone,
so I thought I'd take it off.

I don't know if the comforts of others —
the man who visits fabric stores to play
with bolts of silk that ask for nothing
when he's estranged,
the woman who test-drives cars
she'll never buy to feel
the annointed engine fire —
apply to those who don't know how to live or die.

Still, my friend has given me a memory
expansion board of turquoise pools
and resilient springs,
a thing outside myself to hold
whatever sharp endowments
I choose. And I choose the trees

harboring little pneumatic drills
outside my window, trees infested
with the fricative fuss of small soft birds
along Le Forge. "Le Forge Road —
Isn't that where people go
to dump old stoves?" a man asked at a party.
Yes, and where they come for frication
in the front seats of foreign cars,
their drunken consonance
riding on the wind to me.

I don't know if drivers in those lively confines —
where windows rise electrically,
wipers wave at misplaced knees,

and rear defrosters sap the battery —
find ease, a soft exchange
that's more than fabrication, but I like to think
they might: those drivers who remove their synthetic
permanent press suits
to remove their suits of fire.

The Cutting Bed

I've doused myself in citronella and gone out
to find this country
blemished with ephemera

left by lovers while the others slept.
While others slept, a lover purged himself
from rural route to cutting bed.
His trashed anger — dirty anniversaries,
raw Hallmarks, a cocktail napkin
mushed with come-ons — slips
into the plain brown wrapper of the late
June ooze. So love becomes this

lewd and usual punishment.
Cold fusion. The rose laced with plutonium.
The breeder reactor down the street.

A girl with downcast blush
gives a boy a heart on a stalk
while he grasps a bunch of long-stemmed hearts
behind his back. "Hi Handsome,"
it reads. "You wanted some pussy . . .
So here's some pussy . . .
willow. Ha! Ha! Love, Cindy."

You'd half expect such markers
to give way to bodies. The crude Lucite heart engraved
with "Love" and chained in velvet spelling

"Little Gallery" on the lid
could lead to Cindy dead and dressed
as the med-flight R.N. she writes she was
"definitely ready to be!!"
In the small hours of spring, sheet lightning

opens up this splurge of wrecked commemoratives
left by one who hoped to solve his problems erotically
beneath brown-corseted trees.

Although it's not polite to point,
I can't ignore the past
perfect sometimes homicidal never stingy
bric-a-brac around this house.
From the perennials

a happy grandpa, candy bar in lap, throbs
"Know what they gave on Valentine's Day
before they gave chocolate?

Blow jobs." Cindy's delicate steady hand
continues: "Could I interest you
in a traipse down Memory Lane
to the good old days?" The good old days?
Before mutant bunnies with hearts for butts

were signed "I lust therefore I love?"
When my father wed my mother
because she smelled like honeysuckle?

The Expense Of Spirit

The credits and debits of cold sex:
Release, power, what the back-to-basics fuck-
You on the subway adds up to.

Are we making love yet?

Look, fingers speak and shine the world. They count.
I'd think twice before bagging them
To pass for guns, or cocking
Them through the flesh of some
Likely one whose hand you wouldn't hold.
Endearments ease the deal. Which sounds callous,

Though neither she who guns her reproductive
Engine, whining "Can he be *niced?*"
Nor he who speaks of sex as "making *like,*"
Damning the heart till it rankles, playing with ashes,
Exchange the compliment I mean: to praise the otherness
Rising or widening next to one's own
Nude dilations. We care to an hygienic extent. No more, though
Earth and self get ugly when unloved. Cellulite
Skies where heaven stared! Suffer, but don't let me
See: that's the dearest, cheapest prayer.

The Gilt Cymbal Behind Saints

1. CINDERBLOCK

Once *halo* meant *a threshing floor*.
Once iron flew inward
to form a core.
The crackhouse child

who jammed mixed jive
sang "I want to beast someone,"
pit bulls ripped silver chains
from the heart's skein

while Bloods and Crypts skinned
the siding from prefabs
in the slurbs.
On the playground brick

someone acrylicked
the goofy face of Betty Boop
with pout soured down,
bonneted by a heart

like the gilt cymbal
behind saints' heads.
Her arms beseech
a frowning sun

and clouds that spell
"In Memoriam
Jenny — Evelyn."
Is it a gang's farewell

to hallelujah floozies
from the 'hood? Oh no.
Someone's fixed a cross
corsage to the flat-

finished clouds
and set blossoms
on a cinderblock before them.
Once a house fell

on two children while they played.
And *halo* meant *he cuts away*.
Once shrines were saints
with transcendental lathes

spinning at their napes,
giving comfort
numb as marble.
But the strapless star

whose cartoon mincing
tickled the two kids
is dumbly abrasive.
Build chapels of slab plastic!

Death is always in bad taste.
The parents say their blame
like rosaries. Their search
for cause takes them beyond

slack building codes
to earth's shy core, liable
to raise mountain
chains and plates. Where *halo's*

kin to *loosen*
and *enclose*. A snare
for falling rocks, a coarse
tulle of chain link

drapes the thruway cliffs upstate
in shimmer like cascade.
Twine visible as rain
electrifies as it divides

farm from farm from
wayward touch.
Accidents happen
and police bind the site

with golden tape
to make a gift of space.
Once razorwire whirled
its nimbus through

the diamond surround
of hoops and hopscotch bounds.
Figures seesawed to a tune:
"I want to be loved by you..."

2. CAUSE CÉLÈBRE

Thought God, I crave adoration. Creatures,
Hes and shes, who'll love me 'cause I'm nice.
I'll give them free rein and wavering natures
So just the wise might choose me over vice.

Thus spake Perfection. The gold-ply core
He could have woven in a snap is nowhere
In our tattered selves. The love He's said to roar,
Nothing audible to us. It's the rare
God who needs less stroking than a rock
Star or poetician: the betrayer who's

Betrayed by the crowing of a cock.
In the name of the Father! We can choose
God's heaven where we'll sit around and veg —
Ghostly thrills are dim — or the surrogate
Eternities of earth: art, kids, a hedge
Redux in case *forever's* counterfeit.

There's a double standard for Gods and us:
Humans leading humans to temptation
Are condemned — while the Prince of Ballast
Naps or smiles above our low gyrations,

Brazen in His Emperor's new clothes. "God,
On you it looks good," grovels every prayer.
Truth told, there's no First Cause, but the slipshod
Histories of chance, the planless cascade, the dare

Of gamble are law. If anybody
Flares without a cause it might as well be

Us as God. We hold sway: the cold and warm
Specks in the touch, the go, the form reform.

The Fractal Lanes

Being menial, how can we let vastnesses strike through
Our fastened nerves, or see — being the ordered smallnesses
We are — the whole spill, squeeze, and boiling without
Losing heart, mind, or being
Insinuated — hugged or struck into the unwanted
Northless utmosts, the Southless balconies between
Gables of dust, rotundas of sun? Can it be our comfort's

Derived from our dumbness? It's good to know there are infinite
Exponents within the arrays we've made, that our laws block less
Visible more spectral evidence. Maybe a little
Equity — currently scarved in subterfuge — some
Linchpin — circumspect, magnetic — is yet to be
Opened and made cogent. Practice makes
Pattern. Repeat a thing till the *again*
Sculpts presence. It's some world when

The power leavening each cell's so variously
Hushed that we can't see or hear it. The thrill's in thinking it
Exists as latent prism: the red, yellow, and blue

Rays within a spun concolorous white wheel, the phrases
Interwoven down the left side of some poems, which might stay
Ghostly and unknown till pointed out. Though we base the stars'
Hermetic chemistry upon the light they hurl,
The earth's so close our measures blur. We go by lakes

And rumblings from the core. To think the ground we glide on then
Reside in holds more oxygen than the air! It makes our dying
Meager, too evident for credit — that unreckoned — breadth.

To Each According To His Need

People become as liquid
as possible in times like these.
Junk bonds: If that isn't love it'll have to do.
Worse things happen at sea. The travel ad says
Now you can stretch out all over the globe.
This boy's going to
let the two-oh-nine pacify his mind. This boy's going
to lay his head on that lonesome fabled line.

Smile awhile, I'll kiss you sad adieu,
my mother sang the night of the day
we stole her straight pins, placed them
on the tracks and watched the Silver
Bullet melt them down and Darty Winch, the milkman,

borrowed Daddy's gun from its alligator case.
His horse Sandman drank a little Bud
whenever he delivered to my father's bar
and Darty sang a blues beginning
There's one thing in this world
I cannot understand . . .

Cops came to our door
the night of the day of smoking pins
and Darty Winch, asking if we'd let the midnight special
shine its visionary light on them.
When that drunken Silver Bullet galloped by

birds unraveled in the firmament
the way sheet music should when sounded.
The punch holes in piano rolls also
came to Darty's mind, and the pinholes
people use to view a full eclipse.

The odds the sun would shine
in his back door someday
were like the odds his heart would clench
exactly when the bullet entered nearby. He felt so

inside out. As if his quick
had all come forth unbidden.
He'd never get rich
and dress in polyester suits, never drive
a silver Caddy with whitewalls.
There's one thing in this life

I cannot understand . . .
Do we revolve around the sun or vice
versa? When Galileo chose
to live rather than die, he chose right.
Some truths aren't worth the price.
They'd say he wore a blindfold
and a daunted fedora.

My mother said he'd absconded with funds
and the sister, a bigwig
at The Citizen's Trust, would have to pay.
She hoped he would attain unto mercy.
They never had words, those two.
You're gonna need somebody on your bond,
the sister said. And if that isn't love

it'll have to do.
There's one thing in this world
I cannot understand.
Deep breath. Three Glory Be's.
That's a bowlegged woman
crazy 'bout a cross-eyed man.
Worse things happen

at sea. Now he could stretch out
all over the globe. Go back to those reptiles
who raised sails on their spines
and trapped the sun.
Some had scales that turned to feathers.

He could stretch out, add friends to friends
and find them friends whene'er they met again.
A person becomes as liquid as possible.
A sliver at the bottom of a solvent sleep.

Silencer

When snow soothes the view, it doesn't pay to reason
with each shapely flake of its sinless topsoil.
Better admire the crystal's moronic tolerance.
Better call the proud happy,
the past fixed and finished lives
convicted parts of history.
To live is to be a threshold that persists.

The mind wants to rest its reasons
against the framed snowstorm it keeps inside
the living room, caged in Zenith or something Japanese.
It wants to meditate upon the marrowless Zen
ecstasy that froths between the channels,
to think the moon's the sort of thing
toward which the earth is tending: over.
Over and out. The mind thinks people

die because they have no reason to live or die
for their reason for living since a reason for
living is also a good reason for dying. Then the living
invent more reasonable deaths since the suicides' invention
might be catching. The reason for life might
be to make us want to leave. When friends advise

the mouth to consume more cruciferous vegetables,
the mind to swaddle itself in thermal
thinking, rent a screwball movie,
Pillowtalk, all winter,
the mind thinks something impolite.

Once a force called *she* exists
it can't be made to de-exist.
Though the centuries spend as stuff

before the ongoing (in which nothing's gone
for good) happens to snap cells into something
singular and capable of saying "I"
might be *forever* squared. Welcome
to the blitz indifferent and long-

lived as grit. What a lottery win
it is to live. She was a channel through which
energy traveled in a way it won't again.
But the mind's sugar labyrinths insist
there is a soul: think surround sound
from hidden speakers, think air-
grams, weightless blue. The mind thinks
when death usurps my turbulence that lightening or loss
goes up in soul. It thinks if only.
Then builds tough stuccos of no, ending with no
matter how it waits she won't return.

In the meantime there are common flickers
on the lawn, words to whittle, friends to kid.
In the meantime minds pose and put
each other on with drastic poise.
And though the sun is lustrous
on the snow, minds want to switch on
every watt inside. They want to rest their every
reason against the gusts of blank repose
within their sets and make their blizzard babies.

Losing It

You feel a hard-core blankness
gain the upper hand
while the world turns to glittering
silica, crinkles and rolls
up like a rented movie screen.
The air whirrs: surely
the golden fan that halos saints' heads,
electric and on high,
is rising from your spine.
Before your lips hit the floor
you recognize divestment
and want to dicker, please heaven,
with the slippage, but find yourself
dismissed. Getting lost

was once adventure. As a kid
you and a kindly aunt played at it,
boarding any bus that puffed along, no matter
where it went. Your aunt was mindful
of the transfers, which saw you home
intact. Where is she now
with her calm tokens and cerebral maps?
When your brain's become a Byzantine cathedral

flooded with the stuff of sump and dumpster.
Its frescoes — memories — confetti
into the mortal sludge.
From domes filleted and boned
with light, the impounded soul looks down.

You wake up dumb
as something fallen off a turnip truck
into a new Dark Age. That petrified

river round your legs must be your skirt.
What month? What day? the doctor asks.
Mortified, you lug the answer, a book
dense as a headstone, to your lips.
"I don't know," you whisper.

If brain were body
yours would be unmuscled
and standing in the buff.
The ooze of stupefaction
extends for blocks,
and you have nothing
but a cotton swab
with which to mop it up.
Above the bed, like a sylph
in a filmy sarong,
his head on a plate
of light, Christ sinks
into a blue plush cross.
Pain was never so fey.
Heroic, yet decorative,
he is the way
we wish death to be.
How well he embodies our need
for pleasantry. The oxygen is delicious
as champagne. You wish
to express this dim epiphany.
You'd like to
binge on the fidgety past,
but thoughts sigh slow as elevators
from cell to cell.
And words . . . words are snow
crystals to be grown from vapor.

Outside, the setting sun
dips a straw into the trees

and drinks their green.
This time you are lucky.
You've lost nothing
to speak of: a contact, a way of seeing.

Thinking back on what happened, you imagine
the brain as Byzantine cathedral, flooded
with the stuff of sump and dumpster.
Its frescoes, memories,
confetti into the mortal
sludge. From domes filleted
and boned with light, the impounded soul
looks down.

Then you discard the flood,
which was a kind of comfort; let go
the pan-religious romance of the soul.
What's left — a state
that's strictly ex- and un-,
not-this, not-that, the ne
plus ultra of losing
track: A nothing so engulfing
I had to hide behind
the second person to address it,
as though I spoke of someone

else. I remember my mother
folding my aunt's best blue pajamas
on the empty drawer of her
dresser in intensive care.
If there's a soul it's such
a clingy rayon casing,
deflating almost to absence
when creased in layers of tissue.
From the high ground of health
and self-control, I issued orders to

Try. Her lids, pinned by ether,
strained as she complied.
Squeezing a hand I hadn't
held since childhood, I wanted to forget
myself and beg her to awaken.
Come home, no matter
where you're headed,
the voice inside me said.

The Pivotal Kingdom

A head capsized the wild mechanism of May
and a body followed, casting off
its muddy husk.
I gazed at him from the raised walkway
of the excavation site,
through dust the color of suntan.
I wanted to stroke a thing so warmly
smooth, a uniform khaki, on bended knee.
I wouldn't mind touching hands
tensed round centuries
of hiatus in place of vanished weapons.
His motions tabled for millenniums,
he'd had a long word with the earth.
He'd lodged in its plutonic gut,
an emptiness strung with pulse. Like all mortals,

I have a nodding acquaintance
with the dark.
You know our slogan: Keep it light.
The tiled tunnels beneath rivers, fallout
shelters, the undersides of bridges
where sunbeams slither
like lizards on adhesive toes
are good at holding
shadows. But shadows aren't hard
blackness as much as patterns
made by lesser light.
Even our refrigerators are stuffed
with glow, like well-appointed homes.
Though it's no strain to visit the abandoned
mines beneath Detroit,
the transformers choked in power
lines under Manhattan's tailored granite,
I wouldn't want to lodge

in the clay warrior's dense bed.
I'd miss the inner city
of sensation so solid you'd swear it was
embodied: yearning, an expansive
mansion in the marrow; pain,
a charger of barbed wire;
and joy, a freed slave hoisting
hallelujahs through the nerves.
But is this private sector hidden
in heart or brain or bone?
Does it hold
eminent domain inside our heads, live in
vivid ampules under wraps
of fat, swim through tissue's minnowed shadings,
the opalescent flecks of cellulite
like spectral residues
in flesh? As Socrates said
life's intrinsic
to the soul but accidental
to the body. He said
if the spirit does exist
it isn't a good mixer. In my book
inclusions are not accidents,

though accidents exist.
It's best to conscript them,
the way jazz repeats a slip
till it sounds right.
Just think, it was a mistake
made by plants that created oxygen
and led to us, builders
of plants that change air back
to what our lungs can't trust.
The pivotal kingdom holds

crossbows rigged against intruders,
terra-cotta soldiers guarding

rivers reproduced in small,
and shuttlecocking constellations
at the top. Walking, we're borne
up by glancing blows
that form the ground, spirit cities
fraught with once and future
euphorias, with wars.

Trophies

Over stiff blossoms of cocktails, firm studs of leathered dens,
bucks give perpetuity
above-it-all glass stares.
Their nailed heads must rest secure
their sum lives on the other side
of plaques they wear like pillories.
How wise, how benign they seem.
In contrast to the spiked heads of deposed
dictators, the hors d'oeuvres of history.

Don't trophies mean golden droves of loving cups
incumbent upon glass? Or keepsakes
that preen like sculpted flak,
tureens full of blackout saying the kick in the groin,
the bayonet hung with guts are here made clean.
A tone higher than the note
broadcast by merchants to kill vermin
holds their alloyed atoms intact.
They will last longer than our children,

these vases for bouquets of zilch and zap.
No rosebuds rise like screwed-up lipsticks
from their brass tubes. Brass wombs
they bear transcendence
without blood, pus, piss, spit, snot, or come.
Like children, they cry I won, I won!

Cherry Bombs

At five I knew at twelve
the body's logic
would lead to blood, rah-rah

girly pom-poms, breasts, the secondary sex
signs shaved to lady-
likeness, arrayed in labial

pleats for the world's ease, a skirt
on an escalating gender:
the flatness developed in steps,

a corequake certain
to insinuate me up
despite my fast dissent.

I hated the world's complicitous *give
in, give in.*
Though the shot

silk slips, Lilt perms, and Ambush
scent seemed lusciously adult
a suspicion lingered they were lures

to an unfixable forever
I deeply didn't want.
What did training bras train

breasts to do?
Hadn't I been told
when strangers offered dirty candy

to say no? I said no
to unselective service:
First comes love, then comes marriage,

then comes wifey with a baby carriage!
Prams pulled girls to ga-ga conversations
while boys made GI Joe advances

loving the loud sounds of their mouths.
At the beach I saw
the fate they called "expecting."

Labor was a squeeze and scream
we couldn't play at
making glamorous, like war.

I wanted no part of that combat, no
thank you, no
compulsory unsung heroics, please.

Please immunity. Please a dispensation.
Mother, are there monuments for women
dead of children?

Child, women are the designated weepers
at monuments for men.
But no one engraved spirits

behind the tiny engraved names.
We grew toward an undoing
punctual as mutual.

Boys put on ugliness young:
Filigreed cap pistols
swiveled them to targets,

pulled red strips and banged
on dots of dust
until the air smelled warm

as baking day but different.
Boys trailed their guns like magnets
drawn to polar charms.

Guns swirled like weather vanes
with boys instead of cocks above.
They dropped each other

into herohood, expecting
the chance of bullets
in their flesh, the mold

under their nails, the mold
of uniforms. They saved face
daily, scraping themselves free

of down and drowning
in Vitalis. They turned their hearts
to cherry bombs.

Of age and corseted
in shells, off they went
into the Aqua Velva yonder.

It wasn't that I wanted to be not
female. I wanted to be female
as I was. When another frilly being asked

"Do you have the pretty kind?"
I understood her
meaning: We loved our no-count

cunts and vulvas, though we lacked the words
till high school's titters,
its biology nuns all nuts

and bolts.
"It's what up front that counts"
sloganed the voice-

over selling filtered smokes.
At five I thought the secret
of eternal life was simple

as keep breathing: Out/in.
Girl/boy. Truth/lies.
No one could make me

null and void.
"Would you rather be liquidated
or boiled in oil?"

my sister's witch voice
drifted from the basement.
I thought about it

the rest of childhood, all day.

Home Fires, 1943

Your skin pearled to cirrus
as the belly lump grew upwards.
Or dark streaks fell down your center
that never disappeared. You forfeited the girl
you were, grunting forth the larva of a child. "You think
too much. An infant brings you back to nature. At least give it a try,"
he'd said. As if a child could be *un*tried. You knew there could be no
retreat without a death. How does the song go — "You Can't Say No
to a Soldier"? The drugs made me think I was snapped into
a Dixie Clipper's narrow air, being taxied down the runway
while lights elasticized. "Are you using your
time wisely?" the hostess smiled.

Red exits advertised the emptiness
outside: the stay put or plunge through
acres of God. He came along for the ride.
Not down where he'd see anything, of course. Up.
Up by my head. Push, push push, he said. She's too pushy,
I read. The womb's the body's largest muscle, stronger than a fighter's
biceps. It made me able to turn tables breathing theories through
the rotted flower gas: "He feels gypped once he notices her
power over life. Her trial shrinks him to a goldbrick.
But I'm not built that way, he thinks. I must invent
some transcendental wrangle for myself. The yen
for a womb becomes the yen for a war."

"Stop this agitprop," God roared.
"How many pains make a baby?" I asked.
"Eight to eight hundred seventy-two," he soothed.
"The fetus, a true parasite, will use its host as food,"
Dr. Gutzeit said. Each child a tooth. He had a private practice
galloping through gals' cores with calipers. A snug business, this. I
sang like artillery when I wasn't thinking. Aristotle burned me up.

Telling centuries that the female contribution was a little matter
to which man gave form and life. Years of lady training
went down the drain. You wanted to give him
a swift kick. And Freud, calling birth the start
of anxiety, had the baby in mind.

He weasled the idea from a midwife
who said newborns were scared and flunked
her exam. "Just the facts, ma'am," God declared.
Once the pains rose and the show turned bloody, he asked
to wait outside. He paled at the anguish of anyone he loved.
Well, I thought, a brilliant male who had a son already might find it less
than riveting. Go to the pictures, I told him. "The shadow side,"
Queen Victoria nicknamed it. "Or I'll give you something
to cry about," the hostess griped. And she had nine,
attended by a Mrs. Innocence in her confinements.
When she accepted chloroform — the waves
it caused! For it is written, In sorrow

thou shalt bring forth children.
Then the fetus was thought clay shaped
by the mother's moods to genius or monster.
"Every woman thinks she carries a centipede,"
Dr. Gutzeit believed. And Spartan wives were forced
to siphon war to embryos by focusing on statues of heroic men. I'd read
how women conceived to stay a death sentence and thought All's fair.
I must go now, I told the hostess. I'd rather ship out
to Fort Bliss, buck rivets on B-17s. Oh no,
you want to serve, she said. Desertion's
punishable by death. Death in birth
was such a shame for certain

tribes that the woman and her things
were burned. It's not like death in war.
Though millions died, who's glorified? Well,
I never. Stop that bazooka music! It's boring
through my spine, I cried. For all I'd read I hadn't read

about the bayonets. I tell you, I saw stars. No one will believe me,
I kept thinking. Till a darling-fingered babe with a glance
of slate squirmed like a flame in my arms. How private
his navy iris, a shutter on the interstellar stuff
he was! Grind the skin of a meteor with
a dove's and bathe him in it.
My breathtaker.

Our Calling

To birth shape from the spill

                     To silence is to kill

To raise Cain from the matrix

                     Dislodge   disperse   dispatch —

lifting thoughts from nil

                  the clean words for murder

It's our conspiracy to see

                  Overlord's *a lord supreme*

the world one way

              and code name for the Allied

empire by which we pledge

                  invasion,

allegiance every time we speak

                of Northwest Europe A battle tactic

a narrow anthem by which we zero in

                  is called an Operation

What's disarticulate doesn't exist

                after the knife the blood

Nothing wakes in our head

              that makes us well

unworded The unnamed stateless

                in clean surrounds

sink into the winter page

              we call the theater

unless we carve a clause of granite

                High drama's the standard!

build snug

        Weapons etc.

canons or grand rescue

              are ordnance *from arranging making neat*

At best it's plenty

          The enemy? Never

Its penultimate horizon says

let them choose their names

no zenith   no matter

Christen them Blemish Vegetative

how we reach

Gook Kraut Cunt Zip Slit

At worst lies pit the mother tongue

Gossip stands for tales

like salt on roads

of birth   epics

dry-rot the goddess

songs of war   in short

The world waits for our orders

To man is to make

It haunts

active   To woman? Fill in

our heads   the atomized

the blank

fuzz of gnats

Those icons finding whys

barely there

for war we call

visible only from uncertain

memorials

personal slants

The preferences of men

except that from the swarm

we call our culture   Our end?

we forge our terms

Will beings known as us know all-

except

inclusive death? Oh yes

we call each shot

We call it loss of personnel.

OVERLORD

1. THE EUROPEAN THEATER

During the staging and briefing,
barbed wire, guards held us in a British airdrome
with a plainclothes escort to the mess.
We boxed, played five-card stud
(I lost and won and lost
a Longines watch ten times, the action
was so fast) shot the bull and crap.
Would the thrust be part of a larger squeeze?
Would we succeed?
Hitler's Fortress Europa —
it sounded like a villain's castle from a fairy tale.
We had a condemned man's fancy chow the night before June 5th
while the regimental band played "Holiday for Strings."

The delayed invasion made us jittery as gamecocks.
And since all were trained in hand-to-hand
combat — brother! It was hot.
After the rehearsals we wanted the show
to start. I tried to hold onto my hair
but my buddies ganged me and Geronimo!
The brass showed war pictures to kill time.
Blood lost its bluntness
in black and white and the bombed houses
had no bulk. Still
a hiss and crash inside the hangar
made us rush the door as one.
The first casualties came from this commotion,
caused by a fire
extinguisher falling on a chair.

We were watching a flicker called "Is Everybody Happy?"
when ordered to make ready.
While the others rubbed their mugs with charcoal
I read my sweetheart's letter
asking if I'd changed
my policy in her favor.
I touched the rough butterfly
she'd kissed into the paper.
It made me think
how females paint their faces
for attention, and men paint theirs
to disappear. Thinking I wouldn't
want to die in blackface like a minstrel
I said no
when they handed me the coal.

After the last low Mass
Colonel Johnson's peptalk lodged like mortar
in the crevices of conscience.
Light snapped to attention
on the long blade he drew and raised, saying
he hoped to God he'd plunge it
in some Nazi bastard's heart
before the night was done.
The band played as we stepped smartly off.
Some boys, loaded to the gills
with weight, had to be pushed onto the plane.
They checked our risers, chute, and harness one last time,

issued pills to kill the butterflies.
"I will not bring any of you back
aboard this ship alive," the pilot warned,
patting the holster at his hip.
When the Colonel saw me pale
he said to darken up with engine soot.
Working the exhaust into my skin,

I admired the plane's fuselage,
graceful as a Powers model
in the line of female pulchritude
with bands of black-and-white
distemper to signify her Allied status.
Then everything compressed
began to open, swell, and float
inside my chest: *Oh Lord,*
be near us in the fire ahead.

2. EVE

The V-formation felt intimate, so close
I could have pitched a grenade
onto the neighboring plane.
The fleet penetrated cloud cover, then burst
its shroud and flew in moonlight for a while.
By Golly, it was pretty!
My seatmate played harmonica,
"Don't Sit Under the Apple Tree,"
till I said pucker up, we're coming
to the thick of it.
Some pilots got buck fever,
but we knew the U.S. Navy might pick off any strays.
The ground fire looked like a heaving toppled Christmas
tree. As we began a shallow power dive
it whisked by in arcs brighter than a dance-floor's
mirrored beams. Tracers shimmied up
and fingered tattoos on our tail.
"Jesus, Mary, Joseph,
this baby's going down!"
the pushmaster bellowed.
We stood up, hooked up, and one by one shrieked
out the door. The rule book said relax
and you'll land well. Bullets hit

the chutes like popped champagne.
It's New Year's Eve with noisemakers and streamers.
You're stepping out
onto the dance floor, debonair, your baby's
hand against your neck, her hair —
I said floating down the ladder of flak,
into the small arms fire below.

   3. BED

Oscillating like a maple seed
                          to make a harder target
I lit in water
                          my hips riveted by equipment to the velvet
bed vised in shroud
                          lines struggling for a glimpse of living
                          daylights then a tough silk surface
                          the landscape of chute overhead a guttering
sail dragged face down
lungs flailing like Old Glory
till the wind died
                          a breather shore-leave before
                          downdragged lashed
                          to the plush bottom tonguing the rust
panic sucking on the hum
                          suffocation made a touch and go of stunned
                          ups downs that happened happened helpless as
a hook dragging
the river beating the living
                          daylights out gullet smother spasm lashed
to the plush bed flames drink
                          to the cold draperies of all there is
gypped I had more to live
flames drink all

the oxygen in blackout
                    curtained burning rooms
at last I collapsed
the chute and stood in
                    the tranced aftermath of scared
the false dawn of enemy flares
                    lungs sagging with slag
two spires, a sky-
trooper fluttering
                    banner or gibbeted criminal
from one the red smoke of no-
man's-land: Rouen.
                    I inflated my Mae West and swam.

4. ENGAGED

Against red smoke sent up to say it's us,
a farmhouse formed, clean as ladies'
powder, an honest-to-God girl on the front
steps with a party dress, a red rosebush
by the barn I smelled and smelled
thinking their lives were velvet
before curling up under my innocence.
I slept and woke to a circus

hotter than somewhat by the sound.
Clowns tumbled between risers
in the fields; a jumpmaster spun
the cords from vital bundles like a gay
lariat to attract his men.
The enemy had doused and torched
the house so troopers fell
in curtains of fire.

Rancid scratching fuel and flesh . . .
I got the willies,

pushed my face into a rose,
said "Flash-Thunder-Welcome,"
the password, please open a fairy door to home.
Thinking distant church bells could help
determine my position, I listened
for the Cracker Jack

crickets we'd been issued to chirrup
their kid-stuff signals. I crawled
between wheat and wild-
flowers, thinking God help me
followed by what right had I
to help? I found a little Bible
belonging to a Private Stedd,
carried it and dropped it

on a whim the way the tide drifts bodies
briefly seaward, beaches, buries them,
and starts again.
They'd said to move toward bugles.
That's how eight of us assembled
on the lowing of a cow.
We climbed a bluff and spotted
our armada like a second shoreline,

the sky — so effortless
it looked expendable
above jerry-rigged, shifting roofs of sea.
Just then the Dickman fired,
making the gray beach shiver and ascend.
I'd thought of death as a big nothing
before hereafter started, or else
I'd thought of capture.

I never knew men could bounce
off the ground during bombing
or every elm hiss "Cut me down!"

alive and kicking with sky-
troopers. I never thought a tree could rise
like a spooky fountain,
its boyish gargoyles spewing
out red scrolls —

but there it was, flourishing
its slashed and nasty crop.
Ash, ash, I said and felt
real dumb for speaking
to a tree. Cutting them down
I prayed "Bless us, O Lord,
for these and all thy gifts,
which of Thy bounty we are to receive

through Christ" by mistake
resorting to the mealtime grace.
Most gliders missed their targets
in the dirty night. We passed privates
carrying a GI on a ladder
near one abstract metal mass,
a point man blowing up
a bridge with flashlight batteries,

a wounded trooper yelling "I goofed,
Lieutenant, I goofed . . ."
One ripped face asked for a cigarette
I said I didn't have
not knowing where he'd smoke it.
He wanted to show me the hole
carved and fitted
with a picture of his girl

under crystal in his gun.
Leaving him for German medics
I thought there ain't much
good in the best

of wars these days.
We wondered when *we'd* get engaged. Digging slit
trenches, we fantasized each leaf
flash as a muzzle ready to unzip

our thicket. We fired
grenades at our own forces
while U.S. bombers trained on mine fields
silenced U.S. boys across the hedge.
You got to know the difference
between us and them.
Their weapons sounded like the Library
of Congress being ripped in two.

The bellyaching *nebelwerfers*,
the black ghosts left
by mortars stood for hostiles,
while fire quick as wisecracks
that laid white shields
for infantry meant us.
How lonely it felt
fighting beside strangers only

those in like circumstances know.
By luck, I'd hooked up with some
all-right Joes: no smart alecks bragging
about blasting Jerry to destiny
though one cowboy cried
"Charge!" another "Su-eee!" with a smile
every time he shot his wad.
A shook-up trooper introduced himself

saying "I just impaled a man.
It went in easy but didn't come out
that way." At night the flares
made us feel naked.
Shooting at darkness from darkness

afforded a welcome
privacy till finally
we were caught pants down.

After flirting, it was time
to get acquainted.
When sprayed, the near misses
felt like women's breath.
Then I was swatted
with a two-by-four of steel.
Or a tank took me for dirt, or
some jerk stuck my legs in kegs of fire.

A Jumpin' Jesus, Angel of Mercy,
or pill-roller covered with the cow shit
he's crawled through looms over
offering morphine, fake coffee.
His voice comes from a strange
hard place. I think
I'm stitched from toe to hip.
Nuts. Am I

or am I not
watching a white circle twist
round a black and crippled cross
stuck to his arm, am I or am I
not watching a mailman deliver
through the gate of what was once
a villa to a lady?
A lady waiting for her mail,

although the jig is up:
though there's no villa or drill,
just a slack
hereafter for soldiers
under grayish beams of beach.

Today any man breathing is a man
of means. The easy war
I've had of it till now

flashes by like life:
the staging briefing plainclothes mess . . .
I'm dying
for the infantry
to be jeeped in like kings
and save our skeleton
defense. As the first tank pokes
through a soldier

kisses the sweetheart's
name — "The Only Helen" —
painted on its turret, yells "U.S.
spells *us!*" I bite my tongue
to give myself a different pain
to think of. How beautiful those GIs look
marching up the causeway — like they are
discarding something every step.

The New Old Testament

Autumn's nubile drizzle polishes off the oaks.
The great wars are afterthoughts of brass on bridges,
the monuments, ossified fog.
                              By the bullet-shaped water
tower, in the V between six freeway lanes
a man stands swaddled in granite.
Children think this huge papoose
in his gray gut remembers war.
I, the Lord God, say no —
the trees are better heroes.
Injured, their blond viscera whispers
death rattles only I can hear
and their death takes twenty years.
                              Though small-unit actions
ordered chlorophyll's retreat, the trees' petro-
chemical fire is not rained out.
Though rain laminates the afterbirth of leaves
on earth, a hazardless waste, a propane
spill flaming toward a smothering
of foam, of snow: what wicks, what stoics, the trees.
They are the only Good Soldiers,
                              Good Mothers.
The Women's Relief Corp built stone wedding cakes
in memory of men.
"Such sinews even in thy milk," Ladies,
such stubborn lactose tiers to note such sacrifice.
Your names are the names engraved.
Belle Etcetera, Mary Starkweather.
Belle Etcetera knit bronze into a coat
of arms with rearing bucks, Indian
bearing arrows, a sunrise or set behind him,
a dead tongue cooing, "If you seek
a sweet peninsula look round you." Starkweather

raised a flag-hugging Yankee where bride and groom should be.
This rain is plain acid. Let there be nothing
lovely to it.

The state prison's a tomb that writhes inside.
Those who killed from passion, greed, unsanctioned
rather than in wars deemed civil live there.
Till death, Dear Children, by my hand or yours.
Children forge license plates. They forge prayers
crude as junk mail, each side whining take my side.
"Why hast Thou forsaken me?" Christ sang.
"Fix it up in jigtime," they implore,

"let lightning strike." Least Little Ones,
gnash your teeth till Kingdom Come, I won't be there
to intervene, who would have let the South secede,
Hitler kill six million more.

Trouble In Mind

A murdered body's shallow grave.
A ditch that shelters sniper fire.
Who says memory's a friend? Who'd grieve
to find their sleep unrifled, furred

by a select amnesia? Because I thought
recalling all turned all to sense,
I filed my life in pieces, all that
debris changed to meaning, all scenes to signs.

As soldiers dismember weapons to check
on their perfection, I broke the said
and done. Blame's the bullet you catch
between your teeth or worse, inside.

And if some angel dust or peace
pill, busy bee or killer weed
could turn the past to has-been, a poison
shot let bygones be, who wouldn't

try it? The stuff of Agent Orange
which says the world's no matter, gutting
every ghost within its range.
A jungle of nothing. A forgetting.

The Private Sector

Maybe the afterlife's like August 6, 1959.
I can't remember one remaindered hour
of that day my presence proves I lived through.
Let's say the Good Humor man jingled winter
through our hide-and-seek, handed azure

arctic bars from the truck's safe, making change
while I sang, "Catch a falling star
and put it in your pocket," miming
a visible glitter held by two fingers
tucked tidily away.

Maybe the afterlife's like that
untouted day, lacking
the vexations and radiance
memory keeps
whole between bouts of composure.

Maybe our ignorance of heaven
is the same forgetfulness
that prevents us from detecting what we did
such and such a moment long ago
though vague notions remain — icy messengers

and gates.... As a child I played *Always
Remember*, netting tangent
pageants in my brain. Contempered
by the present, they remain.
Each breath selects

exponents from aggregate
lairs: The past
slims away, wraith

to our séance. Maybe mortality distracts, shrinking
pre- and postbeing to backdrop.

Though heavenly evidence is filched
from hearsay, less
than circumstantial, maybe our ignorance
of any life but this proves zilch.
I know that

ladled into agency,
babies press against the self's
tight faction from day one,
and *Get me out of here*'s the sense
behind their cries. They're trying to

say What?
no migration between ego and amigo, mind and mobile
vulgus? This being me's like being
bricked up in a chimney! Oh yes,
where was I

that certain August 6?
Maybe racing with the big kids,
trying to be in on things.
"They'd let you get ahead
then put on speed," my mother says.

"They never let you win.
When I said stop
teasing, they said 'We can't,
it's too much fun.'" So there
I was and am, legs and psyche

pumping like the Tour de France, believing
in my chance. And the others,
those sisters and winners,

what triggers
the same day in them? A song

by Perry Como moseying along.
The quick souls of ruby-
throated hummingbirds inside the tiger
lilies. Rosita Rubylips,
the witch they scared me with.

I guess anything
hot enough burns
with the same shade flame, no matter
what's on fire. I was the child
who seldom cried, feeling tears

might undermine my dignity. Determined
to be fulcrum, rather
than revolving slave, I made Ptolemy's mistake.
Like a falling star becoming conscious
as it dropped, aware

of motion but unaware of motion's
cause, I assumed I fueled my course.
Trudging through *The Long Portage*,
the dullest juvenile book
in print, I thought the private sector

would emboss it all with gem.
Plaintiffs, face it
when the cascade made the cortex,
it invented dilemma.
When it let brain stems escalate

to plexus, these awkward cressets
on our necks, it created fetters.
There was no pain before imagination:

just the drip-drip of prehistory,
so bland the grandest anima got bored.

Self, you're rigged to feel it.
You're the nonce province,
whose purpose is to know
and dread, the sparked
cargo, who must rebel, expect.

Small Objects Within Reach

It fell to him: a slip,
wrapper, or shift,
knotted and pitched
out a sixth-story window,
a mess of shreds
he might have dodged but chose
to grab: a clump of rags that wailed
in his arms as it hit.

He all but fell himself
seeing he'd waylaid
a little kicking thing with skin
soft as felt.
The hospital said she'd suffered
only bruises: people said
it took a gift
to make that catch,
he must be the seventh son
of a seventh son, and how
could he explain
he'd only stretched
his arms as reflex?

He had to testify
it pestered him.
Wickdipper, women once called him.
Now his synthetic suavity left.
No longer wanting things
he'd lived toward,
he found himself
looking up and running
into others when he walked,
bothered by the birds

that sounded in flocks like metal
hangers on metal racks
in the mall where he was
head custodian. Call that song?
He wanted to lie down
on the sidewalk, all his feelings
put to sleep and laugh
at gravity. Drifting

from his business one day
he saw a woman astride a balcony
railing, disenchanted
with her private prison, wishing
to be disenchained.
Fire fighters idled in the drop zone,
while cops tried to con her
into staying. But the suasions
of space won and she jumped,
exposing the anatomy
of unhappiness, choosing death's ad
infinitum over
desires insuburbium.
"I did it 'cause my parents wouldn't
buy a TV set."
That was her statement
from the rescue net.

High-rise car barns stood
for hills in the flat place
where he lived. People spiraled up
in search of redder sunsets
or better prospects,
like the swash of coming
storms. He drove himself
through steel I-beams,
to see and not be

seen, atop the hive of wheels.
He snubbed all company

but waved at a woman
with her hands full,
whose vision swept
the ground for snares
before each step.
He thought he might as well
join her, the pedestrian
enshadowed by planes and clouds
and cradled obligations.
He might as well
for all the landscape held:
fat smells from fast chains, banks
growing on foreclosures, little spiders
spinning water over distant lawns.

In Appleblossom Time

Mary never cared to bingo all night long
or go on bus trips with the Senior Cits.
When she cleaned she made love
      to the corners, singing I'll be with you
in appleblossom time, as her mother did.
She was at home with a book or visiting
potential possessions in the mall.
      There she met a man in Men's Apparel
from the Sacred Heart parish,
a widower without his glasses.
She read him prices but declined when invited out
      for lunch. She couldn't truly
see a thing in body and ghost
until she felt emotions.

"These days you get propositions
      whatever sex you're in,"
said Mary's cousin Gertrude Wade.
She quoted Richard Lovelace, "Give me a nakedness
with her clothes on," when turning down a date.
      "Suave men make me bilious,"
she'd say. She was one of those family females
who'd sooner cross Niagra on a tightrope
sporting wicker baskets on their feet
      than make the neighbors talk.
Who having mothballed or abashed no end of men,
sustain themselves
with one remembered, one
      exemplary caress.

Mary believed Dante got it backwards
when he wrote "the blessed state rests
in the act of seeing, not in that of love...."

On Singles Shopping Night
at Price Dicer she saw a couple slap each other
beside a Kodak ad for faster film.
The poster showed a diver entering a pool,
        clothed in turbulence
she caused herself, like a waterfall
inside the blue
inhuman. Hear hear! thought Mary. What have you done?
        And those youngsters eyeing each other
beside the Soup for One. In no time no one would be
able to shop without crying.
They'd be appleblossoms, motes in a sunbeam
        in no time. In no time no one.

Everything To Go

It's the Dine-Out Drive-In
where mutant bruiser
trucks gunned by men handcuffed
in tattoos punish the rumble-

strips, and formalin women
on graveyard shifts
feed their kids,
kids, kids.

A tank-topped hitchhiker
jibs, bobs, plays
air guitar nearby.
She primps, applying ptomaine

glares to every snubbing
bumper, and the wide-toothed
comb in her back pocket
marks her as a minor.

"Get in, Fast Food,"
hoots a lead sled of a car.
"I like my ladies cooked
to order and bagged to travel."

"Mister, this ain't Burger King,"
she says. "You don't get it
your way. You take it
my way or you don't get it."

Kids these days, I think.
There's a high-pressure system
over the Midwest
as this clientele that knows

its limits and likes
to exceed them yells
"Everything! To go,"
at loaded intercoms.

"We'll give you a lift
soon as we're finished," I call.
"Yeah, but if some drop-dead
goldcard dude shows first,

I'm a ghost," she says.

The Bandit's Bride

This propulsively entertaining novelette
is written in the form of an interview with a dead woman.
It takes place when the Ice Age was just ending,
geologically speaking, and goddesses
sewn into the heavenly embers of peekaboo gowns
lindied under the baton of Tippy Joyce. It concerns gamblers
whose modestly hopeless wishes made them
risk sums too small to be exciting
on horses too dark to win. I am speaking with my Aunt
Rhododendron, one of the principals.

"At that time there were two high waters in each lunar day.
We lived within walking distance of the savage
scavenger eels that roamed the Hudson River."
                    Thomas Joyce and Opal Fecker.
                    What do those names bring to mind?
"That would be Tippy. Remember how he grinned
above the gents' black ties, the backless infatuations
of the girls? The couples squirming around the floor
like microbes on a slide. I was a biology major
at Skidmore College, one of the Seven Sisters.
I'll say this: he had a way about him.
An in-demand after-dinner speaker. He'd bend dimes
in two with his teeth to entertain the ladies.
The Bowling League voted him Most Pungent Raconteur.
I yearned to exert a sympathetic influence. And I was sick
of balancing the claptrap of his character
like a basket of belongings on my head. Little did I know
I'd spend all three days of honeymoon watching
the sand blow by Blue Mountain Lake!"
                    Isn't that where he met Opal? "My sister-
in-law Rose met her socially and said she snapped
her gum. How often I imagined her

path crossing mine. She'd offer me a stick of Doublemint.
'I'd as soon chew the grouting between bathroom squares,'
I'd sniff. Rose, who was a snoop, glimpsed them
at the window. Forever after I couldn't stop picturing
their silhouettes between the linen
question marks the draperies made.
There was evidence aplenty. I heard
he bought her a muskrat stole.
When John your father offered to pay
for a detective I agreed."

          What did you do when you got the report?
          My mother said you had a temper.
          She said 'Rhoda would stamp her size five feet.'

"The Greek solutions appealed to me.
I wanted to turn Opal to a stone
held by tiny silver claws in a mortician's ring.
Wish her into a spittoon.
I knew Kublai Khan had pierced the hands of women
and strung them from his ships. The Gauls
hung their enemies' heads on their doors
or used their skulls as sacred vessels while refreshing.
I opened the Bible at random for a message.
I prayed there'd be a reckoning
and Tippy would turn penitent.
John your father asked your question.
He said 'Rhoda, what are you going to do?'
You have to understand. Your father was a man
who'd glance at a bankbook and compound his interest
by the hour. I said nothing. I said laylow.
I said the main thing was I wanted to know
did Opal have bobbed hair?
Tippy never let me shingle mine.
John turned the color of Saltines. 'Rhoda,' he said,
'how can you give that so & so houseroom?' Well, how
could a man able to figure his interest by the minute
comprehend I'd have slithered toward my treasure

on my elbows if it helped? I was love desperate."
                    Weren't morals stricter then?
"Clubwomen set the tone. Calliope Gumm (wife of Doctor Gumm
the Glamour Dentist). Stout ladies in costly hats.
They'd appear with shipwrecks, flying
buttresses, aviaries, chandeliers, and fruit
baskets bigger than the ones they brought to
shut-ins battened down with stickpins
on their heads. They were pills, tintypes
or occasionally good eggs
as Mary your mother would say. They cared
whether your service was sterling or plate
and discussed books a la mode. I liked some
they thought impious — *The Bandit's Bride!*"
                    Did you have any hobbies?
"I was interested in the transits of Venus.
Now I speak with posthumous knowledge.
As you travel farther out into the stars,
the number of possible transits increases.
From Pluto you'll see all the planets cross
before the sun. And though I am deceased,
I want you to believe I noticed everything —
from the icy hairnets of December trees
to the quilted skin of strawberries."

Reader, that's the end. There's no crisis or falling
action when you interview the dead.
In a world of limited resources how do you justify
the time you spend, some people say. The answer is
allegiances sneak up. I can't guess how
my subjects feel when set in marbled endpapers,
but I have not regretted it or found better friends.
Grand unified field theories propose
that differences among the forces
will vanish if we probe near enough
to particles experiencing the force
and I've made that my law: the letter and the spirit.

Point Of Purchase

Sermons on unbelief ever did attract me.
Emily Dickinson

How God and billiards originated
no one knows: cases of always
was and will be, I suppose.
Every player has a nickname.
They latched onto my art-passion
and tagged me The Magic Marker.

My mind becomes a coercive crayon

when I shoot. I draw
a thin line from it
to the pocket's center.
Draw another from the cue ball to
infinity. The place the two connect
has a denser gravity, volatile somehow,

and that's the shot. The Billiard Congress

of America started college tournaments
to give the game an ivy edge,
but I'd hate to see it
get respectable. Let it stay
wily as religion, which is based — *I beg to differ*
on pool-shark smarts.

The shriek-green table's comparable

to our volcanic planet.
Humans are those kiddie-colored
slingstones in the rack

73

above which God, our ardent cueman, moves.
They say His spectral beeper keeps Him

everywhere, improbably disguised, like a shyster

trading alligator shoes for a hunter's
hip-high waders, slinkskins
and gold chains for an academic cap and gown
in order to attract a wager.
He might be the old jester
decked in leftover Carnaby Street bells
who comes on like a marching band,
the career criminal in crude
* brown pants crawling with geometry designs.

Or maybe He's those shrimpish figures in the cloth.

I said this to a religious friend who yelped,
"My God's not a midget! My God's big!"
Okay, He's big and we're tattoos
that do the hootchie-coo every time He flexes.

As an artist, I'm influenced by forty-foot stone giants

with vulva symbols carved behind their ears and birds
weighing more than fifty tons of uncertain origins.
Immense and frowning monoliths crowned
with red millstones and carvings
of men with rats in their mouths
found on Easter Island.
I got a grant to visit and witnessed
the force of monuments

like time in overdrive, millenniums subjected to duress,

My sister had a pair of those funky pants

74

given expressions
similar as livery and sutured
to the land. Struck by such
foreverness, I began sculpting in volcanic tuff.
The Polynesians warehouse what they want to keep —
heirlooms, assets, pagan tablets
their recent Christianity outlaws — in secret
storage caves guarded by ancestral ghosts.
Nothing is adhesive. Theft is endemic,

thought a virtue rather than a crime.

A REBELLION AGAINST THE DOMINANT ECONOMIC AND POLITICAL ORDER BASED ON CAPITALIST EXPLOITATION?

Steal trading, it's called in anthro-slang,
but The Pascuense language has words:
hakamaroo (ha-ka-mahr-OH-oh) — to keep
what you're loaned until the owner asks for it — and

tingo — to swipe all you desire from a friend

by persistent borrowing.
There's a hidden compliment in this
since only worthy things are taken.

It's like the contango of hereafter

where God snakes the good away
with promises of reunion.
It's a different sense of turf,
less fixed and more communal.
That culture left its mark on me
as I learned during my chill out
at the artist colony. But I'm wandering
from my topic: God and pool.
Heaven is like the little winnings
hustlers return to crippled suckers,
just enough to let them sputter from the dead.
It's what they call a walking stick.

This bit of slang will date rapidly

> I wish she would!

I can relate
To it. She
reminds me of
my sister, "The Convincer."

The sacraments are draw shots meant to move us

toward God rather than away.
I wish we had some means of depleting
His *vox stellarum* charm —
given that the epochs most mesmerized
have been most hugely cruel —
from Inquisitions to victimized witches.
Historically, organized religions
have been the (backwardation) — *The language calls attention to itself — like a woman wearing too much make-up*
of the human race, centers
for the Dissemination of Intolerance,
squashing every progress with a brute hooray.

They strangle the rafters

where our minds might dwell. Still,
coaxing God into my corner's
become a habit when I play.
Say we *don't* pray. God gets sorry
for Himself, starts erupting with this poor-mouth stuff
on how He's been betrayed.
"Your words have been stout
against me, saith the Lord."

THE DOMINANT WORKSHOP MODE OF READING INSISTS UPON A "TRANSPARENT LANGUAGE THAT DOES NOT ITSELF PRODUCE ANY MEANING BUT REPRESENTS THE MEANING OF THE WORLD AS UN-OBTRUSIVELY AS POSSIBLE." "CULTURAL POLITICS OF THE FICTION WORKSHOP" — MORTON & ZAVARZADEH

Oh, the Infinite has store

and to spare of paranoia.
When it comes to praise
He's like a junkie with a hungry arm.
He gerrymandered heaven into burlesque
echelons, legislated a True Value
Paradise above the filibustering
✱ bitumen of hell.

✱ Once smashed me it, her face twisted like a five when she talked (my sister)

And Christ. Let's hold Him accountable

Give it a rest will ya?!

for a second. Remember the Gadarene swine?
He put devils in those pigs
that made them rush into the drink
when He could have put those devils anywhere.
Would The Humane Society acquit Him?
How about the time He wanted figs
and the tree couldn't deliver,
"For the time of figs was not yet," the Bible admits.
Well, He got vile-tempered as a shark with piles,
put His Eveready hex on it
until it scurvied to a twig.
And who made the tree with its seasons

if not Jesus? (Was it Bertrand Russell

I stole this from?) The indignant sage.
There are people more decent. I mean
Mother Theresa! When you think about it,
Jesus had a mean streak.
His teachings convinced millions
of rank-and-file despairing, presumptuous, unrepentant,
obstinate, argumentative, or envious
souls they'd sinned against the Holy Ghost
and would spend forever in His Duracell Hell
"where the worm dieth not and the fire
is not quenched." By threatening
misbehavers with this cosmic Shake 'n Bake,

He gave the world excuses for the tortures

it wanted to endorse.
Those who questioned His teaching
He deemed vipers, serpents. And suicides
could not be buried in consecrated ground.

"It is the curse of greatness

[handwritten annotation:] now I know how de ayatollah felt!

[handwritten annotation:] This is clever, I suppose, but also trivializing. I must say I dislike this speaker. I feel she is unfair to Christ. High-spirited, but a bit egotistic and noisy... a kind of nervous narcissistic complacency... I look forward to her middle-age say.

77

She should know the answer. This is flip, like a village atheist's blasphemies.

that it must step over dead bodies
to create new life...." Is that Thomas Aquinas
or Heinrich Himmler? If you recall, Saint Thomas
said heretics who find the faith
and then backslide
should be taken into penitence
but put to death.

"THE ZEALOT IS A MAN WITHOUT IRONY. HE IS NOT INTERESTED IN WIT." "TWO CHEERS FOR BLASPHEMY" THE NEW REPUBLIC

Every Sunday my mother drives my former now moribund

ballet teacher, Siena La Tendresse, to Mass.
One day she said, "Annie, I have a secret
that will surprise you.
I might not go to heaven.
You have no idea
what I've been up to in my life." What —

I also thought the speaker was a man up till this point!

have I got a murderer in my car? Ma thought.

Well, in her youth Siena fell in love
with a Protestant choreographer.
Her family objected so strongly
she gave him up and married Harv, a Catholic
baker, on the rebound. She wore widow's weeds
when her first sweetheart died,
though they hadn't seen each other in some
fifty years. Another time

she said, "Annie, I dasn't confess

this to the priest, but when
I met Lionel, my second hubby,
at a Knights of Columbus function,
he spent the evening feeling my thigh
under the table. Was that mortal or venial?"

I do hope humans are too asinine

to be the brightest form of life.
On Memorial Day my mother visited the cemetery
with her suggestible friend, Nell Crandell,
who stood there chanting,
"Now this plant is for all of you,"
as if the dead were learning-impaired
kids. Later she said, "Annie, do you think
my mother and father and daughter and the others

will know the one big geranium is for them all?"

*"THERE IS NOTHING AND NO ONE IN THE WORLD, AS SCIENCE DEPICTS IT, IN WHICH WE CAN HAVE FAITH OR TRUST, ON WHOSE GUIDANCE WE CAN RELY, TO WHOM WE CAN TURN FOR CONSOLATION, WHOM WE CAN WORSHIP OR SUBMIT TO — EXCEPT OTHER HUMAN BEINGS."
— KURT BAIER*

And not them either!

"They must," Ma said.
"You told them enough times."
But imagine the groggy faith
of thinking her family lingers in The Oakwood
waiting for the living to bring tributes.
What by-and-by does that suppose?

I've heard it said the devil made the world

when the good Lord wasn't looking.
But that's the same old dualistic dice toss
of unwisdom I don't buy. I don't know
what clinched it, but I was undeluded
very young. The church lost me
at the point of purchase.

*"THE WRITER IS ALWAYS THE CREATIVE PRODUCER WHILE THE READER IS THE PASSIVE CONSUMER."
"POLITICS OF THE FICTION WORKSHOP"*

It was a bludgeoning sort of

Back at ya!

style over substance
as far as I could see.
During First Communion practice
the Father wanted our palms set
vertically together like a gift-shop

overstock of The Praying Hands.
"No birdcages," he kept saying.
My dreams were demure
consignments: the prettiest crystal rosary, an ivory
missal. Only nuns used beads
plain as lentils.
Holy water came in simple flasks
with a little dirt sifting
at the bottom. Yellow fraying

palms crossed like swords

behind the frames of pious pictures,
the Infant of Prague wore imperial
satin-doll ensembles.
There was a shop downtown devoted
to His clothes next to a place
for people who wore used.

I remember how beggarly the public-

school kids looked when they visited
for religious tutoring, how unkempt, how unlike
us in our parochial blue serge.
I got lost in the rules.
When I was five I cowered in the statued dimness
of the school until waylaid
by a major nun who asked where I was going.
"I'm lost," I said.
* "I'm lost, *Sister*," she corrected.
We were taught to imagine

the soul at birth as a white showroom

Chevy and grace as our Rust-Oleum.
I told my mother how the Sisters of Mercy

80

[handwritten annotations:]

"Don't get me started on that," she used to say. "Once I get started I'm like a raccoon washing a sugar cube till there's nothing left." I wish I could send her this poem.

why don't you buy her a Hallmark!

*I couldn't help my sister. She said once "If a mirror starts to fall, let it. Never try to catch it."

appointed boys as guards and monitors.
They exalted boys to minipriests
like the cosmic wire-pullers with the power
to forgive they'd come to be.
There was one thing I loved:

a coloring book of empty robes and halos

*She was a raging
art beast. She
Thought all sorrows
could be understood
if you made them
into paintings.*

the nuns used as a muzzle
when the priest appeared.
Then we pressed sinuosities
of flesh and goldenrod between
firm black lines for several minutes.
I never finished one whole page
except in my imagination. There
I made the Virgin's vestments plaid,
fastened spike heels to her sandals.
No irreverence intended.

I thought of it as my vocation — to electrify

— hurts the ears, like a

her dowagiac garb.

*deconstructionists
neologism*

But when Sister Denise asked what we wanted to be
I said, "a barmaid." I was "bold,"
a shameful trait in females,
though my back talk was all accident.
Once a priest rasped, "none of your lip," grabbed
my hair and slapped my face in one gesture, ambidextrous

as a Jesuit. Then he hid behind Jesus,

saying, Do you not remember
how He drove the money
changers from the temple
with a whip? In high school priests prowled
the halls like truffle hunting poodles

on the sniff for all the perfume
we weren't allowed to wear.
I was always being told,
Shorten your hair, lengthen your skirt,

be different and fit in.

If you ask me, Christianity's a form of greed.   *Will somebody*
It wants (a) a just universe,   *hose her*
(b) a point to life, (c) all our wishes satisfied. *down?!*
I'll take none of the above.
I'm attracted to more flexible, let's say disaffected
premises, a truth full

of unpragmatic bafflement, open to correction yet

prophetic, so wide and various it's all
but useless. It won't make you live
forever remembering everything. And that
brings me to this: Who needs gonads in the ozone!
God's an It not a Him: complex,
perfect, but without meaning
even for Itself, like the star of Bethlehem,

an asterisk on the outskirts of what seems

                                  hysterical, light-
the point, a crystal   *headed verse, no*
spined with a phantom figure   *feeling at all, only*
like the backboned fanfare   *chattering metaphors*
of star sapphires or constellations,
a little wedge of perfection that shames

the mildewed living, the more exemplary membrane

                                   "THE 'CLEAR,' 'CONCISE,'
that makes our rebellious jellies *AND 'LEAN' STYLE...MAKES*
seem contemptible, but — and here's the rub, *SURE THAT THERE*
                                   IS NO INTRUSION BY
LANGUAGE ITSELF," THUS, "READING/WRITING IS A MERELY
TEXTUAL EXCUSE FOR READER AND AUTHOR TO
82   *RELATE TO EACH OTHER AS TWO INDEPEN-*
       DENT CONSCIOUSNESSES OUTSIDE ALL CON-
       TINGENCIES OF HISTORY — OUTSIDE LANGUAGE
       AND OTHER INTERRUPTIONS." IBID

capable of saying so. At the heart of all
beauty lies something inhuman.
I stole that from Camus.
No crystal becomes extinct
or vindictive, but It is unthinking.

What Emily Dickinson said

about a gun applies: It has the power
to kill without the power to die.
It's the scrim, scam, serene flimflam
that makes whim-
worshipful fools of us, droolers
after proof of furtherance. A haven.

A Stormport: "A heaven

for artists," endowed by a banker
eager to share with a fellowship
of finite, redeemed spirits
was where I wound up once.
I hadn't been there two weeks
when the requisite specter appeared
like a museum's outdoor fountain,
straight yet frayed at the top,

and shackled in luminous boots.

I was sitting naked in the common room, waiting
for my clothes in the Maytag when I glimpsed it.
The others suffered from ghost fear.
They believed in goblinism.
The folkways of Easter Island put me at ease
with spirits, most of whom have lost

their bearings in some lax dominion.

[Handwritten annotation at top:] I have no more sense of knowing the poet here than I would a man running for comptroller with whom I'd spent three hours. Language as a smoke-screen. So much colored dishwater that's labelled "DRINKABLE." I mean 5 of these am/im words?

[Handwritten annotation middle-right:] I read the above comments with no small appreciation. I will now stop reading the poem, and thanks for the advice!

[Handwritten annotation bottom-right:] Although my sister was often obnoxious she was really a good kid. "Lay her down where the sun pours longest in some sweetheart land." We put that on the stone.

At Stormport the living
read *Charlotte's Web* or *The Lord
of the Rings* aloud before bed. It was easy
to regress when little picnics appeared
on our steps like bribes
from the Brothers Grimm.
Whether it was this or what
I'd picked up from the islanders,

when my fellowship ended I said, "A little while,

and ye shall not see me:
and again, a little while, and ye shall . . ."
which gave them lots of gossip.
They'd figured me for an odd one
from the start. But they curled back
into their ruts of shade and song
till something wondrous happened,

a touch of clash

DIDN'T CHRIST SAY THIS? IT WILL PROFIT NOTHING TO TEACH THE ZEALOT ABOUT THE "UNRELIABLE NARRATOR," TO PLEAD THAT THE SPEAKER BECOMES WHAT SHE ABHORS, THAT SHE IS MAD, THAT ART INVENTS.

I'd reconstruct like this:
The artists took on a tragical aspect,
* and dinner no longer clattered
with the bad Italian they liked
to practice. At breakfast
they stared bemused
at all the cheerful food
till one said, "I think I'm cracking
up," and the rest gazed, fascinated,

as at an exposed and molting fresco.

"Or someone is changing
my paintings. I do the edge
in blue one day and by the next

*Once at the dinner table my sister sang "Can I get a witness?" and sank down on one knee.

it's edged in red."
To which the others chorused *Yes!*

I was lipreading at the window

when the director caught a glimpse
of me — thin from living
on nature, and impenitent I admit.
"You mean you never left?" he said.
"*Mais si* and verily.
I slept most days in storage bins.
At night I came alive to shoot
some pool and sneak into the studios."
I seized the chance
to discourse with the artists
while he called the cops.

a double agent?

"I've got (Cezanne's) spirit in my brush,"

Wouldn't Minnesota Fats be more appropriate?

I told them. "I'd consider your efforts,
think this one's eligible
and paint a few red stragglers in.
Others I just neated up.
Beat the sheep from the goats
with equal and remedial dealings
so to speak, a topspin kind of
thing. Now you look at me
as if my chromosomes
were criminal. You look
very pleased. Well,
you congealed boom babies
should be grateful

She'd leave the other artists with no memories of their own to die in...

I didn't paint little unicorns

all over or sell your stuff
at the supermarket as cents-off

specials. Grateful I didn't slip
bee venom in your hidden vodka.
'God does not assign the divine
shitwork to wimps,' Ralph
Waldo Emerson said that I think.

If anything changes, people get sick.

Sociology uses chi-square
to prove it. Think of me shrink-wrapped
and tranked out in some correctional tank,
behind the eight ball with a lady's aid
as you rusticate between Broadway

and betrayal at the heart

of the derriere-garde.
Beam me up, Scotty," I said,
as victim and agent, I was led away.

I bet their dreams changed

to insomnias of me
rappelling down on tackles
shed from heaven, tooling round
their studios on skateboards forged
of lunar light
till gaining purchase,
I worked my sure repair and simulcast
my assets — hidden, liquid, solid, floating, firm
unto the canvas —

to make my vision manifest in them.

If I may indulge in a little recreational prophecy: this poem will never see the light of day

THE READER/VIEWER IS TAUGHT HOW TO 'OBEY' 'AUTHORITY' — HOW IN OTHER WORDS, TO 'FOLLOW' THE INSTRUCTIONS OF THE WRITER/ARTIST.

Except for the distraction of the guy next to me biting his nails, snapping his watch, cleaning his bifocals and cursing as he read, this was an enjoyable poem.

86

Concerning Things That Can Be Doubted

Uncle Jim tried to sue The Good Samaritan
Hospital for selling his blood
to the Red Cross, which didn't seem so odd
once I'd studied medicare and Descartes,
who supposed all we know
might be the doing of an evil spirit
bent on our deceit.
In thinking that his blood was changing
into money, Jim might have been
one of those "certain lunatics"
with brain "befogged by black vapors of the bile,"
who "continually affirm . . . that they are clothed
in purple and gold while they are naked,"
that they are gourds, or that their heads are clay,
their bodies glass, also
cited by Descartes. But it seemed unlikely.

Jim knew gourds were to be had
cheaply at the A&P and brought them home
for Rose, his eighty-year-old wife
to wrestle into edibility,
though this labor made her little
hands shake for several days.
As a child, my sister said Rose
had the softest touch, as if without bones,
making her eyes mist over.
"That's the nicest thing
anyone ever said to me," she sighed.
When their only son was born,
Jim expected Rose to jump and run
at every whimper.
"Tell him there was no Star
in the East," my mother huffed.

And Jim never thought his head was clay,
despite his love for hunkerish TV
religions that claim the body's
so much mud and dust.
He threatened to cut Little Jimmy
off without a nickel if God came on
strong, leaving it all to Oral Roberts.
When I wondered what that preacher's siblings could be
called — Nasal? Anal? — Jim said, "Missy,
I don't like the spirits
you're in business with." But he chortled
telling how Rose's legs seized up
after he drove ten hours straight
on their vacation rather than pay
for a motel. He liked women
he could conscript
as cooks or nurses and saw red
when Little Jimmy married happy
shopaholic Glenda. I think I'd be

like glass, a brittle invisible
solid, if vitreous
light didn't shape me into this
opaque, but my stocky uncle believed himself
quite firmly soldered to his flesh
and blood. "Don't buy anything
from my brother. He's a sharper,"
my father always said.
Though if Little Sisters of the Poor
came begging at his market,
Jim claimed he sometimes gave them something
stale. After Rose died, he ate mystery
dinners of beets and pie filling
from unlabeled cut-rate cans
or supped at The Paradise,
dumping jars of mints in his pockets

since they didn't give him enough food.
He would get his
due. Of course, he wouldn't pay

to die in hospital. Should my mother find him
she was not to summon help
but come back later to see
if he still breathed.
Either he was reconciled
to death or like Descartes believed
there was no sure way
to distinguish waking life
from sleep, making all states
much the same. In the end,
he left the bonds to Jimmy, banking
on his offspring's grudging ways with cash.
And Glenda spent them
to have her breasts reduced and tummy tucked,
paying doctors to cut off
all that flesh, that blood.

A Union House

A different chintz, plush as a blown-up hothouse,
argued from each carpet, wall, and chaise,
turning modest lodging into wraparound tropics.
Bolts, the dry rose of powder in a compact,
draped the blinds, hibiscus sprouted on the spread,
ferns incised a divan where doilies crept
like ground cover over spots especially worn,
and squiggly living plants evaporated in the swarm.
This was The Phoenix, my father's only garden.

Weighed down by room keys strung like smelt,
he mopped as if his swab could gild each fault.
He bore silver kegs into the cellar and the bitter
draught scaled frigid pipes, burst forth in gold shatters.
Roomers left him envelopes of personal effects
as security when they had nothing else: Lockets.
Wedding rings. Gems and junk were given
back at once and no one was evicted.

Stoutly stylish Mrs. Anderson kept house.
She wore hats trimmed with flora and fauna, corsets
made to order, and dozed off with food on her fork.
Her mild heart dribbled quirkily
the day she knocked to find the transient
— like a chastised schoolboy flourishing
his tongue, his eyes the saucer eyes of things pent
up in night — hanging, as if there'd been no point
wide as the point beneath a dancer's toe to bear his weight.

By dark the blinds were seamed with fire from bales
of light behind them. The Phoenix fueled
the hope of slaves before emancipation;
the close sod cellar sheltered their escape.

My father, who believed the sun had cause
each time it fell through casual windows, posed
that happy folklore, though the walls' dark rings
and chains told tales of people caught and wronged.

But Dad's hotel became a sanctuary
in his mind. So he was standing sentry
when a dapper fellow buzzed the desk,
produced a gun, and asked for rags and dust,
for rocks and tin, by which he meant hard cash.
Afraid the thief would find the strongbox flush
or a shooting ruin business, Dad swore Cap Graves,
the police chief, lived next door, lured the burglar to the river,
and with brimstone diction took his mind off murder.

My father thought he'd never die with silver
in his pocket. He worked to keep us solvent.
Coke and 7-Up arrived in wholesale caseloads,
a ticklish liquid candy that made wise kids
befriend us. I wrote with golden pens
that told the hotel's name, and under linens
bought in bulk we slept like mortal fallen ghosts,
"The Phoenix" stitched in red across our breasts.

Blue Laws

Sundays of diligent rain and that
goes double for the snow,
we ate mild white food along the lines
of macaroni and potatoes.
Burglar bars guarded the convenience stores;
gears paused in the closed shop
where my aunt labored weekdays.
Solid-state stood for things that worked
without space — unlike the eyelet
awning of a bridge, torn
between the blue above and river.

All over town, kids hated
the guts of Sundays.
Only lovers handcuffed in sweet
nothings and mothers
who'd cornered the market
on all's well wore smiles.
When the air grew mentholated
in November, trees showed their claws
and people said it was good
sleeping weather.

My aunt had had it
up to here with the heart,
collapsing and filling like a wind sock.
We crossed an optimistic drizzle
of steel — the Congress
Street Bridge — to reach her.
A lucky mind believes
(what event disproves God's love
to priests?) the world is just.
A restless mind's a thief of mercy.

When the obits editor phoned I said that
in the midst of general merriment
she fell upon her sword.
Thank you for sharing that

had not become a catchphrase yet.
As mentioned, we went hand over hand
across ladders of thread
to reach my aunt. *Heavens,*
there was nothing you could do!
That's the dispute. I could testify
to the efficacy of guillotines
for home use. To be mute

while you're flayed
and love is rationed, to take that
desolation, without door or cause
between the terror
and as is . . . *This is*
the life the people
in my childhood sighed
before they ran to sleep.
Come in if you're beautiful,
my mother cried and cried.

For In Them The Void Becomes Eloquent

Dusting under nuptial covers,
the virgin working for the matron
wondered what love had been. A light
housekeeper, she tried different accents. Sixteen.
She stressed the light
in her job title, made believe
she was in charge of bits that drill the dark
for those at sea. A *light*house keeper, she.

The virgin borrowed her mother's vacuum, that was how
she got the job. How she made the windows quiver

like drops about to fall.
Ammonia smelled mean
but left no streaks. It grieved her to think
bright banisters continued
while humans would be dead in seconds.
Once she'd worked for a Home: the old stowed away
their mashed potatoes in the dresser drawers.

God was infinitely excellent,
thus sin was infinitely bad, the Little Sisters said.

The forever fire was precisely right
as punishment, being eternal
but no longer than eternal.
God couldn't lose for winning, she observed.
In Him the void became eloquent, a sound

without knowledge, too high to be heard.
The vacuum's beige fury burned the dust.

It swelled like a male thing:
sooty grouse or lizard. Boys wearing autopsied light
shows for clothes were her firm favorites.
She'd work two hours for four dollars
to buy their latest, play and play it
till she had the lyrics
written in her hand.

One day light would scalpel into grooves
and make a cleaner music.

She'd discover new foods — Gruyere cheese, whole wheat,
learn to say "quiche," get a Visa
and be gone to stay.
Ammonia smelled mean but left no streaks.
Her mother thought this was beneath her.
Yet her mother's vacuum was what she needed
to turn down

the dark like nuptial covers,
to vivisect the night with her bare hands.

Cusp

Sometimes when night turns me transparent
I want to lie on the dispassionate ground
and make of earth a gurney
till dawn lets me be opaque.

Knowing indifference is earth's
common constituent, I can take comfort
in a coldness innocent of aim,
expecting no finesse and no affection, sink
all clamor in the caulking
that's our planet, a little weather-
stripping against space,
and be glad for density,

which lets one substance hold its place
to the exclusion of another:
the pen stay separate from the hand,
the body independent of the earth,
the skin allow no ingress,
and jail and lighthouse
fail to occupy the same terrain.

So the wings big enough to lift us
are too big for us to move!

So the soul's not stashed inside the skull
like a daffodil spring-loaded in a bulb!

Should I be grateful I escaped
pernicious heavens
when acceding to the empty
forms of affirmation might be better
than embracing disbelief?

Give me a minute while I think it through.

No cause for despair. Clinging to a planet
spinning twenty miles a second round the sun
with fourteen pounds of atmosphere
stuck to every mortal inch
and winds of ether streaming through
each cell, how could we not be well?

To the North, the Great Lakes are lit
by towers held to rocks with iron rods.
The glass hives in their heads
breed chips of glow to swarms
that slice night's infinite regress.
In winter, swags and valences of snow
turn the railings cosy as a curtained home.

By sight alone I'd never know
that ice is cold. How can I see
a cloud's less distant than a star
unless the cloud should intervene
between the star and me?

        We recognize what's closest by its power
        to obscure what's far.

Some loveliness is porous as the hush
between notes that makes up music,
the waves of hue that strum the eye,
sensations that chime
through recessed nerves, leaving
the surface undisturbed
as air allows a beacon, flash-
light or light-
house to part the dark on either side.
But only our solid abundance lets us touch.

Electrons make way for a caress.

They want our bodies to be roomy
and float through each other, forgetting,
if forces ever knew or could forget,
that the particles in flesh are dense.
The more we press the more our substance
tries to dodge duress and finds it can't,
which comes across as touch.
How odd that the body's deep resistance
lets us feel another's presence,
and our presence is bestowed
by means of protest too.

That sensation is a failed escapement!

And touch won't prove congruency:
if certain nerves are spooked
we'll feel stroked though we're alone.
Still, no harm supposing
light massages prairies with appeasement
since it neither rips nor pushes them away,
that the swishing blank expanse
of snow comes down to dust ruffles
and each knapsack of quanta
in the atom knows its role.

"I," the erogenous cusp
of mind and world, sees the rose
lining of a bird's beak
and calls the dawn a churchly blue.

But I need lessons in deportment.

How, at three A.M., to find the silo
by its denser cylinder on dark,

refract the husk until it grows
in deeper contrast to the night
and night becomes a positive
beside that lighthouse without light.

Romance In The Dark

The Other, a nebula:
dust that shines, umbrella
in the stars' rain. We study night's curricula
wondering, is it shelter? What specula
can pry such presence? Without flagella
along each fiber, with a flotilla,
please, of sparks: the tarantella

of heaven in our vessels. Such bravura
infuses the contra-
dance of sex. One becomes a mantra
in the other's head, and one mere coloratura
on the outskirts of real song: an amphora
filled with come. Slip and bra

and tie and briefs: we shuck each other of corona
with our clothes. He could use a strict antenna
bent on common sense. She could use a wise duenna
to say star-exposure burns the retina,
cautionary tales: like the one about the ballerina
who crashed down on china

feet. That dancer lacked utility.
And her partner had plenty,
which provided full immunity.
When love becomes a bounty-
hunt, a panty-
raiding prop of boys' virility
or gilt-edged opportunity
for girls to bed down a commodity,
one becomes a party

to obliteration: then women are currency
exchanged between men; men, women's agencies

of power. It's bad policy
to want trust, courtesy,
the occasional, wayward ecstasy.
To see the other as a galaxy
whose spiral arms will cosy
us in privacy

is pure romance. *Nebula* can mean opacity:
so star-struck visions spot affinity
where none exists. Wanting electricity,
we settle for fidelity,
at last admit civility
will do. Lovers swap their dirty
generative wet for the neutrality

of showers, chose to wallow
in autonomy, dismissing the hollow
between breasts as a shifty pillow
at best. We forget a nebula's yellow
glow's bestowed by stars nearby. Solo,
there's no shine. Who'll provide a furlough
from self except our fellows?
Who'll switch the body's gallows
to a willow's
limber swing, lend a halo,
exchange light between hello-

goodbye? Yet I won't falsify
love as simply dreck or heaven. If I vilify
the high risk or glorify
the mortal mess, I fail, though I mollify
the child within, whose end will justify
her needs. The needs I can't deny.

I'll acquaint myself with zero
by way of you before I'll narrow

down to self alone. I'll borrow
darkness, even, as a matt for light. No hero,
I need the chiaroscuro
of another to help me see tomorrow.

Behavioral Geography

The constancy of rainbows — or gypsum,
the nineteenth century's "petrified mist" —
some trick of light or distance,
made me think Niagara Falls
gentle as a crinoline and slim
enough to ford.
Statistics enforced discipline.

They say the first explorers charted all
they hoped to find: tranquil breezes, courteous seas,
beauties equaled by impossibility.
Only a wonder country
could meet such expectations.
And miracles are no criteria
for the everyday.

Mercator, equator,
what's the use!
Our analytical engines go full-tilt
to make the world
look one way to us all,
Euclid freed
of every flaw.

We think reason works
best when left unchecked
by ecstasy.
So a tree beglamored by autumn
sun seen in the blemished rays
of history turns out to be
the hanging tree.

I wanted to define here, there,
and get back home intact. Believing maps

blocked access to influential realms,
I sat an inch from you,
saying, "Who goes there?"
awkward in the face
of all I didn't know and must

suppose. I filled in the blanks
with dragons, found hobgoblins
in the stop and go.
And you became pervasive,
a wandering monument to every major
nonevent. So zero
raises the value of a sum times ten.

I cling to wishful visions
like someone clinging to a tree, complaining
that the tree won't leave.
Hope springs up in me.
Lost, found, bewildered,
when will I learn
to like unsettling transits,

to use the universal
corrective of the sky,
a continental drift
with nothing fixed about it?
Once a woman dressed in wood
lunged down the falls,
as if her flesh were not

irreparable, and lived.
The beauty's the impossibility. Proving?
All views are seasoned
subjectivities, beds
carved by freshets,
warps of the heart.
Ecstasy has its reasons.

Art Thou The Thing I Wanted

These unprepossessing sunsets
and aluminum-sided acres
retain us like problems
more interesting than solutions,
solutions being perfect

lots of condos, the groomed weather
of elsewhere. Well, we must love
what we're given, which is why
we get stuck
on the steel-wool firmament

of home. Since it's the nearest
partition between us and what,
we choose to find it peerless.
And maybe why we wish
to lean our heads on the dense rocking

in a particular chest, as if the only
ocean lives there or a singular wind
swarms where that heart begins.
Sometimes a passing friend
becomes a mascot in our lives,

day in, day out. The thought of this anybody
affects us like a high
pollen count, inspiring a suffering
not unto death, but petty.
Having a crush is the expression.

And we do feel pushed over, compressed
by chaperones we half-asked for.
Take me, take you. Say someone quips

"Your favorite so-and-so got drunk
and said to say hello," I accept it

as a secular blessing. I glow.
Glorious things of thee are spoken!
There should be a word for you
muses of unreason, like "vector"
since vectors have magnitude

and direction without a physical presence.
And the second meaning is "carrier
of infection." Don't we resent
the way our minds circle
unfavorable terrain for easement,

like jets above imagined runways?
Yet we like to be immersed, no sweat, in solutions
cooler than 98.6 degrees,
which explains the lure of fantasy.
"You never wanted," people say accusingly,

as if glut were gladness
rather than a bargain struck.
But what comes to live here — burrs
through clay, brown negligence —
comes to live without

certain fertile perqs. High-tension
wires droop their rules
between harsh Eiffels in our yards.
Eyesores at first, they quickly become
backdrops whose presence nests

in every residence unseen.
And when a line falls, the field sizzles
for a million inches without a sign

of flinch. Yesterday the elder
out back up and tumbled.

It wasn't hit by wind or lightning,
which made the sight of it — suddenly
half hanging on the barn
like a besotted lover on an arm —
more frightening. The trunk was hollow,

devoured by some tree disease.
In a few hours the limbed fluttering
looked normal on the lawn,
and its jagged profile fit
this make-do neighborhood of farms

run in the ground by agri-biz:
The three wilted pickups
in the yard, the tire of rusty geraniums
and sign that reads Beware
of Dog where there's no dog —

the tree looked right
at home among them, metaphorically
on its knees. Like others,
I mistake whatever is
for what is natural.

You know the commonplaces. How people think
women are good
at detail work when that's the only work
they're given. Or how
the city's invisible

engines jiggled our coffee
till we believed quivering a constant
property of liquid.

Everything happens to me, I think,
as anything reminds me of you: the real estate

most local, most removed.
As on the remains of prairie
the curving earth becomes a plinth —
from which we rise, towers
of blood and ignorance.

ACKNOWLEDGMENTS

Arete: From "OVERLORD:" "1. The European Theater," "2. Eve"
The Atlantic: "Powers Of Congress"
Boulevard: "The Expense Of Spirit," "Romance In The Dark"
Epoch: "Concerning Things That Can Be Doubted," "Losing It"
Gettysburg Review: "Disorder Is A Measure Of Warmth"
Grand Street: "Cascade Experiment," "Everything To Go"
Michigan Quarterly Review: "Hardware," "Small Objects Within Reach"
New American Writing: "Our Calling"
The New Republic: "The Orthodox Waltz," "Trophies"
Ontario Review: "The Private Sector"
The Paris Review: "Art Thou The Thing I Wanted," "Cusp," "For In Them The Void Becomes Eloquent," "Silencer"
Partisan Review: "The Pivotal Kingdom"
Poetry: "A Union House," "Self-Storage," "Trouble In Mind"
Poetry East: "Behavorial Geography"
The Yale Review: "The Fractal Lanes"

Poems were reprinted in the following anthologies:

The Best American Poetry, 1988, John Ashbery, ed. (Collier Macmillan, New York, 1988), "Losing It."

The Best American Poetry, 1989, Donald Hall, ed. (Collier Macmillan, New York, 1989), "Powers Of Congress."

The Best American Poetry, 1991, Mark Strand, ed. (Collier Macmillan, New York, 1991), "The Fractal Lanes."

The Best of the Best American Poetry, 1988–1997, Harold Bloom, ed. (Scribners, New York, 1998), "Powers Of Congress."

Arvon International Poetry Competition, 1987 Anthology, Ted Hughes and Seamus Heaney, eds. (Arvon Foundation, Devon, England, 1989), "4. Engaged," from "OVERLORD."

New American Poets of the '90s, Jack Myers and Roger Weingarten, eds. (David R. Godine, Boston, 1991), "Cherry Bombs," "Powers Of Congress," and "Self-Storage."

Writing Poems, Robert Wallace and Michelle Boisseau, eds. (HarperCollins, New York, 1996), "The Orthodox Waltz."

Roth's American Poetry Annual 1988, H. Weintraub, ed. (Roth Publishing, Great Neck, New York, 1989), "Trouble in Mind."

Roth's American Poetry Annual 1990, (Roth Publishing, Great Neck New York, 1990), "Cascade Experiment."

Roth's American Poetry Annual 1997 CD-ROM (Roth Publishing, Great Neck, New York, 1997), "Trouble in Mind" and "Cascade Experiment."

Seasonal Performances: A Michigan Quarterly Review Reader, Laurence Goldstein, ed. (University of Michigan Press, Ann Arbor, 1991), "Hardware."

Wherever Home Begins, Paul Janeczko, ed. (Orchard Books, New York, 1995), "Everything to Go."

"A Union House" and "Self-Storage" were awarded the 1989 Bess Hokin Prize by *Poetry*.

I'm grateful to Andrea Beauchamp and Barbara Petoskey for lending a hand with "Point of Purchase."

I wish to thank the John Simon Guggenheim Memorial Foundation, the Ingram Merrill Foundation, the Michigan Council for the Arts, and the Michigan Society of Fellows for the support that helped me to write the poems.

THE AUTHOR

Alice Fulton's other books of poems include *Felt, Sensual Math, Palladium,* and *Dance Script With Electric Ballerina.* A collection of essays, *Feeling as a Foreign Language: The Good Strangeness of Poetry,* was published by Graywolf Press in 1999. She has received fellowships for her poetry and essays from the John D. and Catherine T. MacArthur Foundation, the Ingram Merrill Foundation, and the Guggenheim Foundation. Her work has been included in five editions of *The Best American Poetry* series, as well as in *The Best of The Best American Poetry.* She is currently Professor of English at the University of Michigan, Ann Arbor.

Photo by Robert Turney